Linda Patterson

Reference Photos for Artists

Selected Collection of Flowers

Contents

Introduction   1

Pictures For Your Inspiration   2

Downloads   46

Thanks   47

1

Introduction

This collection of beautiful flower pictures carefully selected for your inspiration. It's a comprehensive compilation, created for use as reference in your paintings and artwork. This book full of handy images and would be helpful for any kind of artist; there is no doubt that you would find the right image you're looking for. All pictures are licensed under Creative Commons Zero which means you can freely use in your paintings without asking any permission or providing any attribution. All those images are available in extra high resolution and you will be able to download them any time by the link at the end of the book. Enjoy!

2

Pictures For Your Inspiration

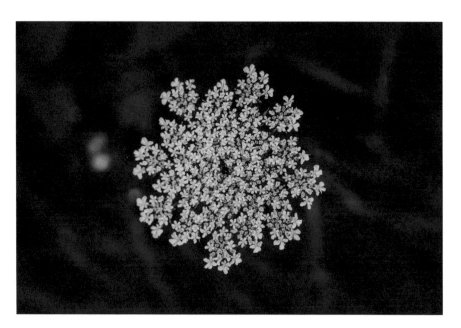

3

Downloads

All resource from the book are available by the link https://goo.gl/C2X65o.
Those images licensed under Creative Commons Zero, so feel free to
use them for reproductions, prints and whatever you want!

4

Thanks

Thank you for choosing "Reference Photos for Artists: Selected Collection of Flowers". If you enjoy this photo book, please consider leaving a short review on Amazon, or share it with your friends.

As always, your support encourages and motivates me to produce more high quality content for you.

Printed in Great Britain
by Amazon